INDIANA
SCIENCE
FUSION

Assessment Guide

Grade 2

HOUGHTON MIFFLIN HARCOURT

Printed in the U.S.A.

ISBN 978-0-547-45162-6

 2 3 4 5 6 7 8 9 10 0982   19 18 17 16 15 14 13 12 11
4500300590   BCDEFG

Contents

Unit 1 The Practice of Science

Unit 2 Matter

Unit 3 Motion and Forces

Unit 4 Weather and the Sky

Unit 5 Life Cycles

Unit 6 Designs to Meet Needs

ISTEP+ Practice Tests

Overview

ScienceFusion provides parallel instructional paths for meeting the Indiana Revised Academic Standards for Science. You may choose to use the print path, digital path, or a combination of both. The quizzes, tests, and other resources in this Assessment Guide may be used with any path you choose.

The *ScienceFusion* assessment options are intended to give you maximum flexibility in assessing what your students know and can do. The program's formative, summative, and performance assessment categories reflect the understanding that assessment is a learning opportunity for students and that all students must demonstrate standards mastery at the end of a school year. Indiana has reduced the number of science benchmarks in the Revised Academic Standards for Science, allowing you to spend more time on the shorter list of topics. With fewer standards to cover than in previous years, the assessments are also very focused and concise.

Formative Assessment

At the end of each lesson in the Student Edition, the Brain Check will help you evaluate how well students grasped the concepts taught. The opportunities for students to annotate their Student Edition, including the Active Reading features, can also provide insight into how well students are learning the concepts.

Opportunities are provided throughout the program for students to check their progress and understanding. At the end of each digital unit, a student self-assessment prompts students to return to areas in which they may need additional work.

The Teacher Edition offers a number of additional tools for formative assessment. Look for the science note-booking strategies Generate Ideas and Summarize Ideas that begin and end many of the two-page sections of the lessons. These strategies provide numerous ways to informally assess whether students are remembering what they read and getting the main ideas. Questions that address a variety of dimensions—including concept development, inquiry skills, and use of reading strategies—are strategically placed throughout each lesson. Located in this Assessment Guide is yet another tool, the Observation Checklist, on which you can record observations of students' ability to use science inquiry skills.

Summative Assessment

To help you reinforce and assess mastery of unit objectives, *ScienceFusion* includes both reviews and tests. You will find the Unit Reviews in the Student Edition. Lesson Quizzes and Unit Tests are provided in this Assessment Guide. All of these assessment tools are in formats that mirror the ISTEP+ assessment formats. Also included in this Assessment Guide are ISTEP+ Practice Tests that provide items for all the science standards in the Revised Academic Standards for Science.

Performance Assessment

Performance tasks provide evidence of students' ability to use science inquiry skills and critical thinking to complete an authentic task. A brief performance task is included in the Teacher Edition with each Unit Review. A more comprehensive performance task is provided for each unit in this Assessment Guide. Each includes teacher directions and a scoring rubric.

Self-Assessment and Portfolio Assessment

Students should be challenged to reflect on their work and monitor their learning. Several checklists are provided for this purpose. Self-Assessment—Active Reading, Experiment/Project Summary Sheet, Self-Assessment—Science Notebook, Science Experiences Record, and Guide to My Science Portfolio can be used by students to describe or evaluate their own experiences and projects. Opportunities for self-assessment and evaluation are embedded at key points on the digital path.

Online Assessment

All of the quizzes and tests within this Assessment Guide are available in computer-scored format with the *ScienceFusion* online resources. Banks of items from which tests can be built are also available.

Test-Taking Tips

Understandably, students often experience test-related anxiety. Teaching students to apply a number of general test-taking strategies may bolster their confidence and result in improved student performance on formal assessment. As students take a test, they should

- scan the entire test first before answering any questions.

- read the directions slowly and carefully before beginning a section.

- begin with the easiest questions or most familiar material.

- read the question and all answer options before selecting an answer.

- watch out for key words such as *not, least, best, most,* and so on.

- carefully analyze graphs, tables, diagrams, and pictures that accompany items.

- double-check answers to catch and correct errors.

- erase all mistakes completely and write corrections neatly.

Test Preparation

Students perform better on formal assessments when they are well prepared for the testing situation. Here are some things you can do before a test to help your students do their best work.

- Explain the nature of the test to students.

- Suggest that they review the questions at the end of the lessons and the chapter.

- Remind students to get a good night's sleep before the test.

- Discuss why they should eat a balanced meal beforehand.

- Encourage students to relax while they take the test.

Performance Assessment

Teachers today have come to realize that the multiple-choice format of traditional tests, while useful and efficient, cannot provide a complete picture of students' growth in science. Standardized multiple-choice tests cannot fully reveal how students *think and do things*—an essential aspect of science literacy. Performance assessment can provide this missing information and help balance your assessment program. Well-constructed performance assessments provide a window through which teachers may view students' thought processes.

An important feature of performance assessment is that it involves a hands-on activity in which students solve a situational problem. Students often find performance assessment more enjoyable than traditional paper-and-pencil tests. Another advantage is that it models good instruction: students are assessed as they learn and learn as they are assessed.

Performance Assessment in *ScienceFusion*

Performance tasks can be found in two locations in *ScienceFusion*. In the **Teacher Edition,** a brief performance task is part of the information that accompanies each Unit Review. In this **Assessment Guide,** a more comprehensive task follows each Unit Test. Both types of performance tasks will provide insights into students' ability to apply key science inquiry skills and concepts taught in the unit.

Administering Performance Tasks

Unlike traditional assessment tools, performance assessment does not provide standardized directions for its administration or impose specific time limits on students, although a suggested time frame is offered as a guideline. The suggestions that follow may help you define your role in this assessment.

- *Be prepared.*
  A few days before students begin the task, read the Teacher's Directions and gather the materials needed.

- *Be clear.*
  Explain the directions for the task; rephrase them as needed. Also, explain how students' performance will be evaluated. Show students the rubric you plan to use, and explain the performance indicators in language your students understand.

- *Be encouraging.*
  Your role in administering the assessments should be that of a coach—motivating, guiding, and encouraging students to produce their best work.

- *Be supportive.*
  You may assist students who need help. The amount of assistance needed will depend on the needs and abilities of individual students.

- *Be flexible.*
  Not all students need to proceed through the performance task at the same rate and in the same manner. Allow students adequate time to do their best work.

- *Involve students in evaluation.*
  Invite students to join you as partners in the evaluation process, particularly in development or modification of the rubric.

Rubrics for Assessing Performance

A well-written rubric can help you score students' work accurately and fairly. Moreover, a rubric gives students a better idea of what qualities their work should exhibit before they begin a task.

Each performance task in the program has its own rubric. The rubric lists performance indicators, which are brief statements of what to look for in assessing the skills and understandings that the task addresses. A sample rubric for a task in this **Assessment Guide** follows.

Scoring Rubric

Performance Indicators

_____ Assembles the kite successfully.

_____ Carries out the experiment daily.

_____ Records results accurately.

_____ Makes an accurate chart and uses it to report the strength of wind observed each day.

Observations and Rubric Score

3	2	1	0

Scoring a Performance Task

The scoring system used for performance tasks in this **Assessment Guide** is a 4-point scale that is compatible with those used by many state assessment programs. You may wish to modify the rubrics as a 3- or 5-point scale. To determine a student's score on a performance task, review the indicators checked on the rubric and then select the score that best represents the student's overall performance on the task.

4-Point Scale			
Excellent Achievement	Adequate Achievement	Limited Achievement	Little or No Achievement
3	2	1	0

How to Convert a Rubric Score into a Grade

If, for grading purposes, you want to record a letter or numerical grade rather than a holistic score for the student's performance on a task, you can use the following conversion table.

Holistic Score	Letter Grade	Numerical Grade
3	A	90–100
2	B	80–89
1	C	70–79
0	D–F	69 or below

Developing Your Own Rubric

From time to time, you may want to either develop your own rubric or work together with your students to create one. Research has shown that significantly improved performance can result from student participation in the construction of rubrics.

Developing a rubric for a performance task involves three basic steps: (1) Identify the inquiry skills that are taught in the chapter and that students must perform to complete the task successfully, and identify what understanding of content is also required. (2) Determine which skills and understandings are involved in each step. (3) Decide what you will look for to confirm that the student has acquired each skill and understanding you identified.

Classroom Observation

"Kid watching" is a natural part of teaching and an important part of evaluation. The purpose of classroom observation in assessment is to gather and record information that can lead to improved instruction. In this booklet, you will find an Observation Checklist (p. AG xiii) on which you can record noteworthy observations of students' ability to use science inquiry skills.

Using the Observation Checklist

- *Identify the skills you will observe.*
  Find out which inquiry skills are introduced and reinforced in the chapter.

- *Focus on only a few students at a time.*
  You will find this more effective than trying to observe the entire class at once.

- *Look for a pattern.*
  It is important to observe a student's strengths and weaknesses over a period of time to determine whether a pattern exists.

- *Plan how and when to record observations.*
  Decide whether to

  —record observations immediately on the checklist as you move about the room or

  —make jottings or mental notes of observations and record them later.

- *Don't agonize over the ratings.*
  Students who stand out as particularly strong will clearly merit a rating of 3 ("Outstanding"). Others may clearly earn a rating of 1 ("Needs Improvement"). This doesn't mean, however, that a 2 ("Satisfactory") is automatically the appropriate rating for the rest of the class. For example, you may not have had sufficient opportunity to observe a student demonstrate certain skills. The checklist cells for these skills should remain blank under the student's name until you have observed him or her perform the skills.

- *Review your checklist periodically, and ask yourself questions such as these:*

  What are the student's strongest/weakest attributes?

  In what ways has the student shown growth?

  In what areas does the class as a whole show strength/weakness?

  What kinds of activities would encourage growth?

  Do I need to allot more time to classroom observation?

- *Use the data you collect.*
  Refer to your classroom observation checklists when you plan lessons, form groups, assign grades, and confer with students and family members.

Date _____

Rating Scale			
3	Outstanding	**1**	Needs Improvement
2	Satisfactory	☐	Not Enough Opportunity to Observe

Names of Students

Inquiry Skills											
Observe											
Compare											
Classify/Order											
Gather, Record, Display, or Interpret Data											
Use Numbers											
Communicate											
Plan and Conduct Simple Investigations											
Measure											
Predict											
Infer											
Draw Conclusions											
Use Time/Space Relationships											
Hypothesize											
Formulate or Use Models											
Identify and Control Variables											
Experiment											

Using Student Self-Assessment

Researchers have evidence that self-evaluation and the reflection it involves can have positive effects on students' learning. To achieve these effects, students must be challenged to reflect on their work and to monitor, analyze, and control their own learning—beginning in the earliest grades.

Frequent opportunities for students to evaluate their performance build the skills and confidence they need for effective self-assessment. A trusting relationship between the student and the teacher is also essential. Students must be assured that honest responses can have only a positive effect on the teacher's view of them and that responses will not be used to determine grades.

Two checklists are found in this **Assessment Guide.** One is Self-Assessment—Active Reading: a form that leads students to reflect on and evaluate their role as active readers. The second is the Experiment/Project Summary Sheet—a form to help students describe and evaluate any projects or activities they may have designed or conducted as independent inquiry.

Using Self-Assessment Forms

- *Explain the directions.*
  Discuss the forms and how to complete them.

- *Encourage honest responses.*
  Be sure to tell students that there are no "right" responses to the items.

- *Model the process.*
  One way to foster candid responses is to model the process yourself, including at least one response that is not positive. Discuss reasons for your responses.

- *Be open to variations in students' responses.*
  Negative responses should not be viewed as indicating weaknesses. Rather, they confirm that you did a good job of communicating the importance of honesty in self-assessment.

- *Discuss responses with students.*
  You may wish to clarify students' responses in conferences with them and in family conferences. Invite both students and family members to help you plan activities for school and home that will motivate and support students' growth in science.

Think About It

Are you an Active Reader? To find out, read each sentence. Does the sentence tell about you? Circle "yes" or "no." If you are not sure, circle the ?.

1. I often stopped to think about what I read.   Yes   ?   No

2. When I did not understand something, I put
    a ? near it.   Yes   ?   No

3. I followed the directions for Active Reading
    on each page.   Yes   ?   No

4. I took time to study the pictures on each
    page.   Yes   ?   No

5. I made notes in my book to help me
    remember things.   Yes   ?   No

6. I wrote answers for almost everything in
    Sum It Up!   Yes   ?   No

This is how being an Active Reader helped me.

_____

_____

This is what I will do to be a more Active Reader next time.

_____

_____

Name _____

My Experiment/Project

You can tell about your science project or experiment by completing the following sentences.

1. My experiment/project was about _____

   _____

2. I worked on this experiment/project with _____

   _____

3. I gathered information from these sources: _____

   _____

4. The most important thing I learned from doing this

   experiment/project is _____

   _____

5. I think I did a (an) _____ job on my experiment/
   project because _____

   _____

6. I'd also like to tell you _____

   _____

Name _____

Think About It

Do you keep a Science Notebook? Circle "yes" or "no" to tell about your Science Notebook. If you are not sure, circle the ?.

1. I am making a table of contents in the front
   of my notebook.   Yes   ?   No

2. I am making an index in the back of my
   notebook.   Yes   ?   No

3. I write plans for investigations in my
   notebook.   Yes   ?   No

4. I put notes and drawings in my notebook.   Yes   ?   No

5. I write questions I have about science in
   my notebook.   Yes   ?   No

6. I use my notebook to help me remember
   what I have learned.   Yes   ?   No

This is what I like about my Science Notebook.

_____

_____

This is what I will do to make my Science Notebook better.

_____

_____

Portfolio Assessment

A portfolio is a showcase for student work, a place where many types of assignments, projects, reports, and writings can be collected. The work samples in the collection provide "snapshots" of the student's efforts over time, and taken together they reveal the student's growth, attitudes, and understanding better than any other type of assessment. However, portfolios are not ends in themselves. Their value comes from creating them, discussing them, and using them to improve learning.

The purpose of using portfolios in science is threefold:

- *To give the student a voice in the assessment process.*
- *To foster reflection, self-monitoring, and self-evaluation.*
- *To provide a comprehensive picture of a student's progress.*

Portfolio Assessment in *ScienceFusion*

In *ScienceFusion*, students may assemble portfolio collections of their work. The collection may include a few required papers, such as tests, performance tasks, lab response pages, and Experiment/Project Evaluation forms.

From time to time, consider including other measures (Science Experiences Record, Self-Assessment—Active Reading, Self-Assessment—Science Notebook). The Science Experiences Record, for example, can reveal insights about student interests, ideas, and out-of-school experiences (museum visits, nature walks, outside readings, and so on) that otherwise you might not know about. Materials to help you and your students build portfolios and use them for evaluation are included in the pages that follow.

Using Portfolio Assessment

- *Explain the portfolio and its use.*

  Describe how people in many fields use portfolios to present samples of their work when they are applying for a job. Tell students that they can create their own portfolio to show what they have learned, what skills they have acquired, and how they think they are doing in science.

- *Decide what standard pieces should be included.*

  Encourage students to identify a few standard, or "required," work samples that they will include in their portfolios, and discuss reasons for including them. The Student Task sheets for the performance assessments in this **Assessment Guide,** for example, might be a standard sample in the portfolios because they show students' ability to use inquiry skills and critical thinking skills. Together with your class, decide on the required work samples that everyone's portfolio will include.

- *Discuss student-selected work samples.*

  Point out that the best work to select is not necessarily the longest or the neatest. Rather, it is work the student believes will best demonstrate his or her growth in science understanding and skills.

- *Establish a basic plan.*

  Decide about how many work samples will be included in the portfolio and when they should be selected. Ask students to list on the Guide to My Science Portfolio (p. AG xxi) each sample they select and to explain why they selected it.

- *Tell students how you will evaluate their portfolios.*

  Use a blank Portfolio Evaluation sheet to explain how you will evaluate the contents of a portfolio.

- *Use the portfolio.*

  Use the portfolio as a handy reference tool in determining students' science grades and in holding conferences with them and family members. You may wish to send the portfolio home for family members to review.

Name _____

My Science Experiences

Date	What I Did	What I Thought or Learned

Name _____

My Science Portfolio

What Is in My Portfolio	Why I Chose It
1.	
2.	
3.	
4.	
5.	
6.	
7.	

I organized my Science Portfolio this way because _____

_____

_____

_____

_____

Name _____ Date _____

Portfolio Evaluation

Aspects of Science Literacy	Evidence of Growth
1. Understands science concepts *(Animals, Plants; Earth's Land, Air, Water; Space; Weather; Matter, Motion, Energy)*	_____ _____ _____
2. Uses inquiry skills *(observes, compares, classifies, gathers/ interprets data, communicates, measures, experiments, infers, predicts, draws conclusions)*	_____ _____ _____
3. Thinks critically *(analyzes, synthesizes, evaluates, applies ideas effectively, solves problems)*	_____ _____ _____
4. Displays traits/attitudes of a scientist *(is curious, questioning, persistent, precise, creative, enthusiastic; uses science materials carefully; is concerned for environment)*	_____ _____ _____

Summary of Portfolio Assessment

For This Review			Since Last Review		
Excellent	Good	Fair	Improving	About the Same	Not as Good

How Do We Use Inquiry Skills?

1 What do you do when you use your five senses to learn about things?

Ⓐ classify

Ⓑ observe

Ⓒ record

2 Look at the picture. Paola used this tool to observe eight rocks.

Paola put the rocks into groups that were alike. What did she do?

Ⓐ classified the rocks

Ⓑ made a model of the rocks

Ⓒ made an inference about the rocks

3 Look at the picture. Tuan measures this temperature in the afternoon.

She knows that the afternoon temperature is higher than the morning temperature. What inquiry skill did she use?

Ⓐ classifying

Ⓑ comparing

Ⓒ recording

4 What do you do when you infer?

Ⓐ use what you observe to tell why something happens

Ⓑ compare objects and put them into groups

Ⓒ use a model to find out how a real object works

How Do We Use Science Tools?

1 Look at the pictures. Which tool do you use to measure temperature?

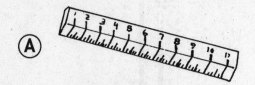

Ⓐ

Ⓑ

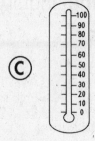

Ⓒ

2 Which tool measures mass?

Ⓐ a balance

Ⓑ a ruler

Ⓒ a thermometer

3 Ana wants to find the weight of some apples. Which tool should she use?

Ⓐ a ruler

Ⓑ a scale

Ⓒ a balance

4 Octavio wants to measure the amount of water his dog drinks. Which tool should he use?

Ⓐ a measuring cup

Ⓑ a ruler

Ⓒ a scale

What Tools Can We Use?

❶ Which unit could you find on a measuring cup?

Ⓐ cup

Ⓑ inch

Ⓒ pound

❷ What do many rulers and tape measures use as a unit of measurement?

Ⓐ inches

Ⓑ pints

Ⓒ pounds

❸ Which object should you measure with a ruler?

Ⓐ a house

Ⓑ a pencil

Ⓒ a playground

❹ Look at the picture.

How is the boy using the tool?

Ⓐ He is measuring the length of his arm.

Ⓑ He is measuring around his arm.

Ⓒ He is weighing his arm.

How Do Scientists Think?

❶ Look at the picture. You want to know more about this animal bone.

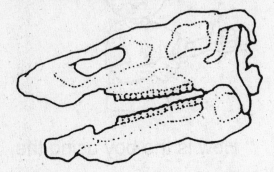

What would you do next?

Ⓐ ask a question

Ⓑ communicate results

Ⓒ draw a conclusion

❷ Anita and Reiko are putting objects into a bathtub filled with water to see if the objects will sink or float. What are the girls doing?

Ⓐ asking a question

Ⓑ doing a test

Ⓒ forming a hypothesis

❸ Which is **true** about a hypothesis?

Ⓐ It must be correct.

Ⓑ You make it after a test.

Ⓒ You can test it.

❹ Jason completes an investigation. The results are not what he expected. What should he do?

Ⓐ change the results

Ⓑ pay no attention to the results

Ⓒ repeat the investigation

How Do We Solve a Problem?

❶ What is a model?

   Ⓐ a drawing or a figure that shows what something is like

   Ⓑ a plan for building something

   Ⓒ a set of problem-solving skills

❷ You want to find out how something works. What should you do?

   Ⓐ draw a conclusion

   Ⓑ make a hypothesis

   Ⓒ make a model

❸ Why should you draw a design before you build a model?

   Ⓐ to have a plan for your model

   Ⓑ to solve a problem

   Ⓒ to test your model

❹ Look at the picture.

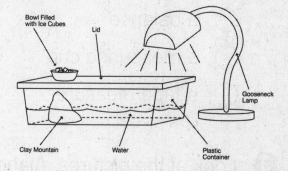

This model shows the water cycle. What is the **main** reason it is a good model?

   Ⓐ It shows how the water cycle works.

   Ⓑ It is smaller than the actual water cycle.

   Ⓒ It uses a lamp to show light from the sun.

The Practice of Science

❶ Jared uses his sense of sight to observe how two leaves are the same and different. What is he doing?

○ classifying

○ comparing

○ making a model

ⓈNature of Science

❷ Bo wants to measure the amount of milk needed for a recipe. Which tool should he use?

○ a balance

○ a measuring cup

○ a tape measure

ⓈNature of Science

❸ Look at the pictures. Alandra wants to observe the details of some rocks. Which tool should she use?

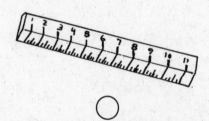

○   ○   ○

ⓈNature of Science

4 How do you know if your test is a fair test?

○ You get the same results each time.

○ You do the same thing to each part being tested.

○ You form a hypothesis that you can test.

Nature of Science

5 Patty puts one plant in the shade and one plant in the sun. She thinks the plant in the shade will not grow as well as the plant in the sun. What is she doing?

○ comparing

○ planning

○ predicting

Nature of Science

6 What do you do when you make a hypothesis?

○ observe how things are alike and different

○ sort things into groups

○ make a statement that you can test

Nature of Science

7 Cal wants to know how much water a container will hold. Which tool is he MOST LIKELY to use?

○ a balance

○ a measuring cup

○ a tape measure

Nature of Science

8 Teresa observes how some rocks are alike. Then she puts the rocks into groups. Why does she do this?

○ to classify the rocks

○ to make a model of the rocks

○ to measure the rocks

Nature of Science

9 Ira wants to find out the temperature of the air. Which tool should he use?

○ a hand lens

○ a tape measure

○ a thermometer

Nature of Science

10 Stu wants to measure the distance around a ball. Which tool should he use?

○ a ruler

○ a thermometer

○ a tape measure

Nature of Science

11 Two students are recording the outside temperature. They use the same thermometer and record at the same time. When they compare data, which will MOST LIKELY be true?

○ Their data will be the same.

○ Their data will be different.

○ Their data cannot be compared.

Nature of Science

12 James and Monique do the same investigation. They get different results. What should they do?

○ do a different test

○ repeat the test

○ throw away the results

Nature of Science

13 How do you know if a conclusion makes sense?

○ It is based on the data.

○ It matches the hypothesis.

○ A scientist writes it.

Nature of Science

14 You use a lot of force to throw a tennis ball. What can you infer?

○ The ball moved slow.

○ The ball moved fast.

○ The ball didn't move.

Nature of Science

15 What is a design?

○ a plan for making something

○ a set of problem-solving steps

○ something that you build

Nature of Science

16 You want to make a model of Earth to understand its shape. Which object is the BEST choice for your model?

○ a shoe box

○ a basketball

○ a paper bag

🅙 **Nature of Science**

17 What is one way a model can help you solve a problem?

○ A model is something that you can build.

○ A model forms conclusions so you don't need to.

○ A model can show how parts fit together.

🅙 **Nature of Science**

18 These pictures are in sequence. How do you know?

○ They show different groups.

○ They show how to share ideas.

○ They show what happens first, next, and last.

🅙 **Nature of Science**

19 You observe that after it rains, there are many worms on the ground. You also observe many birds fly to the ground and begin pecking at the soil. What question might you ask?

○ Are the birds too wet to fly?

○ Are the birds looking for worms to eat?

○ Are the birds eating the soil?

Nature of Science

20 Which is TRUE?

○ You form a conclusion to plan your investigation.

○ You form a conclusion to tell what will happen in a test.

○ You form a conclusion about what you learned from a test.

Nature of Science

Tool Survey

Materials

paper and pencil

Procedure

1 Working with a partner, make a list of measuring tools that you often use. Include such tools as a ruler, a measuring cup, a thermometer, a measuring tape, a clock or watch, and a scale.

2 Next, ask 10 people which of the tools they have used this week. Carefully record this information.

3 Then make a bar graph to display the data you have collected.

4 Compare your results with those of another student pair. Based on the data, determine the three most commonly used tools.

Tool Survey

Materials Performance Task sheets, paper, pencils

Time 25 minutes

Suggested Grouping pairs

Inquiry Skills gather data, record, compare, draw conclusions, communicate

Preparation Hints Before children begin, you may wish to show them a variety of household and classroom tools.

Introduce the Task Have children discuss some tools they might have used with adults at home. Children who have helped with cooking at home might have used tools that measured teaspoons, tablespoons, cups, pints, quarts, and gallons, all of which are units of volume. Distribute the Performance Task sheets, and ask children to read the directions aloud with you. Answer any questions that children raise.

Promote Discussion To extend the exercise, have children divide their interviewees into two groups: children and adults. Have children show the data for each group in separate graphs. Ask children whether they can make the same conclusion about the tools used by each group.

Scoring Rubric

Performance Indicators
_____ Collects and records data carefully.
_____ Accurately organizes the data into a bar graph.
_____ Works cooperatively with classmates to compare results.
_____ Interprets the data to make a reasonable conclusion about commonly used tools.
Observations and Rubric Score
3   2   1   0

Name _____ Date _____

What Are Solids, Liquids, and Gases?

❶ What happens to liquid water when it is heated?

  Ⓐ It condenses.

  Ⓑ It freezes.

  Ⓒ It evaporates.

❷ Which picture shows a solid?

Ⓐ

Ⓑ

Ⓒ

❸ Which is **true** about all solids?

  Ⓐ All solids are hard.

  Ⓑ All solids feel smooth.

  Ⓒ All solids have their own shape.

❹ What state of matter is water vapor?

  Ⓐ a gas

  Ⓑ a liquid

  Ⓒ a solid

How Can Water Change States?

1 What state of matter is water when it falls as rain?

- Ⓐ a gas
- Ⓑ a liquid
- Ⓒ a solid

2 What happens to frozen water when you heat it?

- Ⓐ It condenses.
- Ⓑ It evaporates.
- Ⓒ It melts.

3 What causes water to expand?

- Ⓐ freezing it
- Ⓑ stirring it
- Ⓒ pouring it

4 What happens to water when it evaporates?

- Ⓐ It becomes a gas.
- Ⓑ It becomes a liquid.
- Ⓒ It becomes a solid.

What Are Some Ways to Change Matter?

❶ Which is **true** about cutting?

Ⓐ Cutting causes matter to melt.

Ⓑ Cutting changes the shape of matter.

Ⓒ Cutting makes a new kind of matter.

❷ You make a mixture of sugar and water. What happens to the sugar?

Ⓐ It freezes.

Ⓑ It evaporates.

Ⓒ It dissolves.

❸ What is a mixture?

Ⓐ a mix of different colors

Ⓑ a mix of different kinds of matter

Ⓒ a mix of different kinds of solids

❹ Which is a mixture?

Ⓐ an apple

Ⓑ a bowl of fruit salad

Ⓒ a sliced banana

How Can We Combine Matter?

❶ You do an activity to see how fast different things dissolve in water. How can you record the results for others to see?

- Ⓐ talk about the results
- Ⓑ think about the results
- Ⓒ write the results in a table

❷ Pat adds a spoon of rice to a cup of warm water. How will she know if the rice dissolves?

- Ⓐ It will float in the water.
- Ⓑ It will sink to the bottom of the cup.
- Ⓒ It will mix completely with the water.

❸ Hugo tests salt, sand, and soil to see if they dissolve in water. Which one will dissolve?

- Ⓐ salt
- Ⓑ sand
- Ⓒ soil

❹ Felice put a sugar cube in each beaker. In which beaker did the sugar cube dissolve?

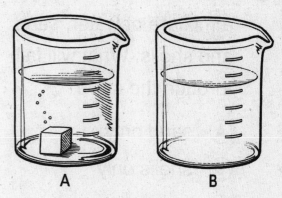

A   B

- Ⓐ Beaker A only
- Ⓑ Beaker B only
- Ⓒ Beaker A and Beaker B

How Can We Separate Matter?

1 How can you use this tool?

- (A) to separate a mixture of rice and water
- (B) to separate a mixture of salt and water
- (C) to separate a mixture of sugar and water

2 You use a sieve to separate a mixture of water, sand, and shells. What will fall through the sieve?

- (A) sand only
- (B) shells only
- (C) water and sand

3 You observe how long it takes to separate salt from water. How can you record your results?

- (A) talk about them
- (B) think about them
- (C) write them in a chart

4 Ana separates a mixture of two kinds of beans. How does she separate the beans?

- (A) by evaporation
- (B) with a sieve
- (C) with forceps

Matter

1 Lola sees a balloon filled with air. She knows
the air in the balloon is a gas. How does she know?

○ The air is matter.

○ The air has its own shape.

○ The air takes the shape of the balloon.

Nature of Science

2 Which word tells about the amount of matter something has?

○ mass

○ shape

○ solid

Nature of Science

3 Which picture shows a liquid?

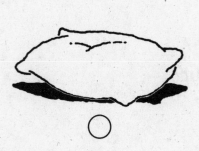      

○   ○   ○

Nature of Science

4 Which is a gas?

○ milk

○ a rock

○ water vapor

Nature of Science

5 Which is an example of water in a solid state?

○ ice cubes

○ raindrops

○ water vapor

2.1.1

6 How is the ice cube changing?

○ It is dissolving.

○ It is freezing.

○ It is melting.

2.1.2

7 How does bread change when it is cut?

○ It changes shape.

○ It dissolves.

○ It melts.

Nature of Science

8 Before school, Tim sees several puddles on the playground. It is a sunny day. After school, the puddles are gone. What MOST LIKELY happened to the puddles?

○ The puddles froze.

○ The puddles evaporated.

○ The puddles melted.

2.1.2

9 When Tina goes to sleep, it is raining. When she wakes up, it is snowing. What MOST LIKELY happened during the night?

○ The temperature got higher.

○ The temperature got lower.

○ The temperature stayed the same.

2.1.2

10 Jonah left a plastic bottle of water in the freezer. When he took it out, the water was frozen and the bottle was bulging. Why?

○ The water evaporated and changed the shape of the bottle.

○ The water expanded and changed the shape of the bottle.

○ The water melted and changed the shape of the bottle.

2.1.2

11 What is the FASTEST way to evaporate water?

○ put it in the freezer

○ leave it in the sun

○ heat it on the stove

2.1.2

12 Look at the picture. It shows a change you can make to eggs.

Which describes the same kind of change?

○ breaking a pencil

○ folding a piece of paper

○ melting ice cubes

Nature of Science

13 Kayla mixes lemonade. Which will dissolve in the mixture?

○ the lemon slices

○ the sugar

○ the water

2.1.2

14 What happens when salt is mixed with warm water?

○ The salt dissolves.

○ The salt floats in the water.

○ The salt sinks to the bottom of the container.

2.1.2

15 You place a sugar cube in a cup of warm water and a sugar cube in a cup of cold water to see which dissolves faster. How can you record your results?

○ talk about your results

○ think about your results

○ write about your results

2.1.2

16 Dad cooks some noodles in a pot of water and salt. He asks Richard to get him a strainer. Why?

○ to separate the noodles from the pot

○ to separate the noodles from the salt

○ to separate the noodles from the water

2.1.3

17 Sal mixes a drink powder with some water. His sister wants to know if the items can be separated. What could they do to separate the drink powder from the water?

○ freeze the mixture to separate the drink powder from the water

○ use evaporation to separate the drink powder from the water

○ use a sieve to separate the drink powder from the water

2.1.3

18 Which mixture do you predict would be the EASIEST to separate?

   ◯ beads and marbles

   ◯ beads and water

   ◯ four colors of beads

2.1.3

19 You have a mixture of soil and water. What is the BEST way to separate the mixture?

   ◯ evaporate the water

   ◯ stir the mixture

   ◯ use a sieve

2.1.3

20 Beth has a mixture of water, ice, and sugar. She wants to separate the substances. She uses a sieve to separate the water and the ice. What should she do NEXT?

   ◯ add more sugar

   ◯ evaporate the water

   ◯ use the sieve again

2.1.3

Comparing Matter

Materials

cotton ball   uncooked macaroni

Procedure

❶ Observe the piece of macaroni and the cotton ball. Look at them and touch them. Write your observations in the chart.

Macaroni		Cotton Ball	
Texture		Texture	
Shape		Shape	
Color		Color	

❷ Are these objects solids, liquids, or gases? Tell how you know.

Comparing Matter

Materials Performance Task sheets, cotton balls, uncooked macaroni

Time 20 minutes

Suggested Grouping pairs

Inquiry Skills observe, compare, infer

Preparation Hints Count out one cotton ball and one piece of macaroni for each pair.

Introduce the Task Tell children that they will compare the properties of two familiar objects: a cotton ball and a piece of macaroni. Ask children to name and discuss the properties of matter, including size, shape, texture, color, and mass. Identify some words children can use to describe these properties, such as *fuzzy* or *smooth* to describe texture. Distribute the Performance Task sheets, and ask children to read the directions aloud with you. Answer any questions the children raise. Tell children that they will be working in pairs.

Promote Discussion When children finish, invite them to share their findings and explain their conclusions.

Scoring Rubric

Performance Indicators
_____ Observes the properties of the materials and records his or her observations in a chart.
_____ Classifies the materials as solids.
_____ Demonstrates understanding through explanation of findings and conclusions.

Observations and Rubric Score
3   **2**   **1**   **0**

How Do Objects Move?

1 What is motion?

Ⓐ the color of something

Ⓑ the movement of something

Ⓒ the position of something

2 Which can move **fastest**?

Ⓐ

Ⓑ

Ⓒ

3 How do the cars on the Ferris wheel move?

Ⓐ in a circle

Ⓑ in a straight line

Ⓒ in a zigzag

4 Which moves back and forth?

Ⓐ a carousel

Ⓑ a slide

Ⓒ a swing

How Can We Move a Ball?

❶ You move a ball to show this motion.

How can you describe the motion?

Ⓐ round and round

Ⓑ straight line

Ⓒ zigzag

❷ You and a friend observe the movement of a ball. Which sense do you use?

Ⓐ sight

Ⓑ smell

Ⓒ taste

❸ You move a ball to show this motion.

———————

How can you describe the motion?

Ⓐ round and round

Ⓑ straight line

Ⓒ zigzag

❹ Amber and Nick observe that one ball rolls faster than another. How could they find out why this happens?

Ⓐ ask their friends

Ⓑ plan an investigation

Ⓒ talk to their teacher

How Can We Change the Way Objects Move?

❶ A boy is pushing a cart.

What happens?

Ⓐ The cart does not move.

Ⓑ The cart moves away from the boy.

Ⓒ The cart moves toward the boy.

❷ What can change the direction in which an object is moving?

Ⓐ a force

Ⓑ position

Ⓒ speed

❸ Which of these forces is a pull?

Ⓐ kicking a can

Ⓑ opening a drawer

Ⓒ throwing a ball

❹ Where is the cat's head?

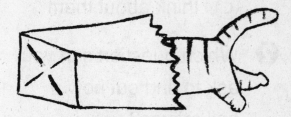

Ⓐ to the left of the bag

Ⓑ in front of the bag

Ⓒ inside the bag

How Can We Change Motion?

❶ You push a toy car. Then you observe how it moves across the floor. How can you record your observations?

   Ⓐ write them

   Ⓑ tell a friend about them

   Ⓒ think about them

❷ Which question can you ask to find out how a ball moves?

   Ⓐ Where is the ball?

   Ⓑ How high can I bounce the ball?

   Ⓒ What color is the ball?

❸ You think that pushing a ball will change its motion. What is the **best** way to know for sure?

   Ⓐ take a picture of the ball

   Ⓑ write a story about the ball

   Ⓒ push the ball to see what happens

❹ What question does the picture answer?

   Ⓐ Who will catch the baseball?

   Ⓑ How far will the baseball go?

   Ⓒ How can I change the motion of the baseball?

Name _____ Date _____

What Is Gravity?

① What keeps the chair on the floor?

Ⓐ air

Ⓑ gravity

Ⓒ the girl

② You let go of a box. What does gravity do to it?

Ⓐ Gravity makes it fall apart.

Ⓑ Gravity opens it.

Ⓒ Gravity pulls it to the ground.

③ What keeps the owl from being pulled to the ground?

Ⓐ gravity

Ⓑ the owl's wings

Ⓒ the tree branch

④ Which is **true**?

Ⓐ Gravity is a force that pulls things down to Earth.

Ⓑ Gravity lifts things off Earth's surface.

Ⓒ Gravity pulls only on things that are touching the ground.

What Are Magnets?

❶ Which kinds of objects does a magnet attract?

- Ⓐ objects made from paper or plastic
- Ⓑ objects made from rubber or cloth
- Ⓒ objects made from steel or iron

❷ Which object may a magnet attract?

Ⓐ

Ⓑ

Ⓒ

❸ Why do these magnets repel each other?

- Ⓐ The same poles are facing each other.
- Ⓑ Different poles are facing each other.
- Ⓒ All magnets repel each other.

❹ Which is **true**?

- Ⓐ A magnet must touch an object to attract it.
- Ⓑ A magnet does not have to touch an object to attract it.
- Ⓒ A magnet must touch an object to repel it.

Motion and Forces

1 Which word tells about speed?

○ fast

○ motion

○ zigzag

2.1.4

2 Which can move the FASTEST?

○   ○   ○

2.1.4

3 What can change about an object when you put a force on it?

○ a pull

○ a push

○ speed

2.1.6

4 What moves the swing?

○ direction

○ a force

○ speed

2.1.6

5 A table-tennis ball bounces back and forth. Which two senses do you use to observe the movement of the ball?

○ sight and hearing

○ taste and smell

○ touch and taste

2.1.4

6 Which lets you move in a straight line?

○ a carousel

○ a slide

○ a swing

2.1.4

7 You and a friend see a ball move. How can you compare what you see with what your friend sees?

○ move the ball again

○ think about ways to make the ball move

○ talk about what you see

2.1.4

8 You move a ball to show this motion.

○

How can you describe the motion?

○ back and forth

○ round and round

○ zigzag

2.1.4

9 How can you make an object move away from you?

○ hold it still

○ pull it

○ push it

2.1.6

10 You roll a car down a ramp. How can you record what you find out about the motion of the car?

○ draw or write about it

○ read more about it

○ talk to your teacher about it

2.1.6

11 How do the children move on the swings?

○ back and forth

○ side to side

○ round and round

2.1.4

12 How is the man MOST LIKELY changing the position of the box?

○ He is putting it under the truck.

○ He is moving it out of the truck.

○ He is lifting it above the truck.

2.1.5

13 What kind of force is on the rope?

○ a pull

○ a push

○ speed

2.1.6

14 How can you find out if a push or a pull can change the motion of an object?

○ You can investigate.

○ There is no way to know.

○ You can weigh the object.

2.1.6

15 What question does this picture answer?

○ What is the ball made of?

○ How can I make a ball move?

○ How many kinds of balls are there?

2.1.6

16 You kick a soccer ball. What puts a force on the ball?

○ the air

○ the ground

○ your foot

2.1.6

17 What happens to the ball when the boy lets go of it?

○ Gravity keeps the ball in the boy's hand.

○ Gravity lifts the ball above the boy's head.

○ Gravity pulls the ball to the ground.

2.1.7

18 What keeps the pen from falling to the ground?

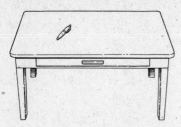

○ Gravity holds it up.

○ The air holds it up.

○ The desk holds it up.

2.1.7

19 Which of these does a magnet attract?

○ paper

○ rubber bands

○ steel nails

2.1.7

20 Two magnets are moving toward each other. What is happening?

○ Different magnetic poles are attracting each other.

○ Gravity is moving the magnets.

○ The same magnetic poles are attracting each other.

2.1.7

How Does It Move?

Materials

ball   book   pencil

Procedure

❶ Jump as far as you can.

❷ Lift a ball off the floor. Then drop the ball.

❸ Move a book across a table or desk.

❹ Tell what forces made things move. Use this table.

Action	Forces
jump	
lift and drop ball	
move book	

❺ Which forces did you use more than once?

How Does It Move?

Materials Performance Task sheets, balls, pencils, textbooks

Time 25 minutes

Suggested Grouping individuals or pairs

Inquiry Skills observe, classify, conduct an investigation

Preparation Hints Clear an area for jumping and for bouncing balls.

Introduce the Task Review forces that make things move—pushing, pulling, gravity—and how each functions. Remind children that more than one force may act on an object. Distribute Performance Task sheets, and ask children to read the directions aloud with you. Answer any questions that children raise. Specify terms that children will use to identify forces in the table: *push, pull, gravity*.

Promote Discussion Invite volunteers to share their tables and to identify the forces that caused each movement.

Scoring Rubric

Performance Indicators
_____ Conducts investigation by jumping, lifting and dropping a ball, and moving a book.
_____ For each action, accurately identifies and records the force or forces involved.
_____ Identifies the force or forces that were used more than once.

Observations and Rubric Score
3   2   1   0

How Does Weather Change?

1 Which object needs wind to make it move?

Ⓐ a bike

Ⓑ a kite

Ⓒ a train

2 Look at the picture.

What is the weather like?

Ⓐ snowy and cold

Ⓑ sunny and hot

Ⓒ windy and rainy

3 Which can change about the weather during the day?

Ⓐ precipitation

Ⓑ temperature

Ⓒ temperature and precipitation

4 Which tool measures temperature?

Ⓐ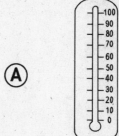

Ⓑ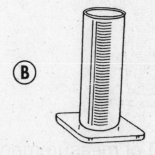

Ⓒ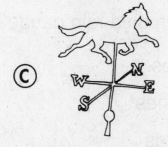

How Can We Measure Precipitation?

1 Which tool measures precipitation?

 (A)
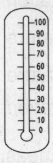

(B)
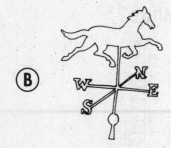

(C)
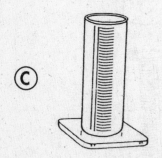

2 What unit of measurement is shown on a rain gauge?

(A) cups

(B) inches

(C) yards

3 You observe and measure the weather for five days. Then you make this chart.

Mon	Tues	Wed	Thurs	Fri
rainfall 2 inches	sunny	cloudy	rainfall 1 inch	sunny

Which is **true**?

(A) It rained less on Monday than it did on Thursday.

(B) It rained more on Monday than it did on Thursday.

(C) The weather stayed the same all week.

4 What can you use a rain gauge to measure?

(A) rainfall and snowfall

(B) rainfall and temperature

(C) rainfall and wind speed

What Are Some Weather Patterns?

1 Which season is usually the coldest?

Ⓐ spring

Ⓑ summer

Ⓒ winter

2 Look at the picture of the water cycle.

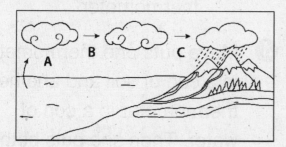

What is happening in Step A?

Ⓐ condensation

Ⓑ evaporation

Ⓒ precipitation

3 Which is **most likely true**?

Ⓐ The air temperature is warmest in the morning.

Ⓑ The air temperature is coldest in the afternoon.

Ⓒ The air temperature is warmest in the afternoon.

4 Which season is the warmest?

Ⓐ fall

Ⓑ summer

Ⓒ winter

Name _____ Date _____

How Does the Sun Heat Earth?

❶ Look at the pictures. Which tool can you use to measure how the sun warms Earth?

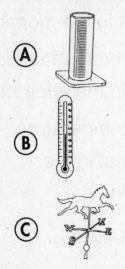

Ⓐ

Ⓑ

Ⓒ

❷ Tony puts a cup filled with soil and a cup filled with water in the sun. He measures the temperature of the soil and the water after an hour. Which question can he answer by doing these steps?

Ⓐ Does the sun heat soil or water faster?

Ⓑ Does the sun heat soil or air faster?

Ⓒ Does the sun heat water or air faster?

❸ How can you **best** compare the temperature of the air and the temperature of a lake?

Ⓐ feel each one with your hand

Ⓑ guess the temperature of each

Ⓒ measure each with a thermometer

❹ Maya puts one thermometer in a cup of soil and another thermometer in a cup of water. Then she puts both cups in the sun. How can she find out which material takes in more energy from the sun?

Ⓐ She can see which one looks warmer after an hour in the sun.

Ⓑ She can measure the temperature of the soil.

Ⓒ She can measure and compare the temperatures of the soil and the water.

How Can We Prepare for Severe Weather?

1 Look at the picture.

What kind of severe weather does the picture show?

Ⓐ a hurricane

Ⓑ lightning

Ⓒ a tornado

2 Which describes a tornado?

Ⓐ a flash of electricity in the sky

Ⓑ a large storm with rain, thunder, and lightning

Ⓒ a spinning cloud with a cone shape

3 Which tool **best** helps meteorologists predict severe weather?

Ⓐ a computer

Ⓑ a rain gauge

Ⓒ a thermometer

4 Where should you stay if you know that a severe storm is coming?

Ⓐ in a swimming pool

Ⓑ inside a safe place

Ⓒ outside under a tree

How Do the Sun and Moon Seem to Change?

1 Which is **true**?

(A) An object's shadow is always the same size.

(B) An object's shadow is always in front of it.

(C) An object's shadow changes as the position of the sun in the sky changes.

2 How is the moon different from the sun?

(A) The moon does not give off its own light.

(B) You can see the moon during the day.

(C) The moon is a star.

3 When can you see the moon in the sky?

(A) only at night

(B) only in the afternoon

(C) at night and sometimes during the day

4 Which picture shows a full moon?

(A)

(B)

(C)

Weather and the Sky

1 Which picture shows an object that is using wind to make it move?

○ ○ ○

2.2.2

2 Look at the picture. What is the weather like?

○ rainy and cold

○ snowy and cold

○ sunny and warm

2.2.4

3 Which tool can you use to tell how hot or cold the air is outside?

○ a rain gauge

○ a thermometer

○ a weather vane

2.2.1

4 Which tool measures the direction of the wind?

 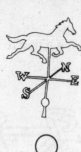 

○   ○   ○

2.2.1

5 Which season usually has the HIGHEST temperatures?

○ summer

○ spring

○ fall

2.2.4

6 How can you stay safe during a thunderstorm?

○ play outside

○ stand under a tree

○ stay indoors

2.2.6

7 Which would you MOST LIKELY observe during a hurricane?

○ heavy rain and strong winds

○ heavy snow and strong winds

○ a spinning cloud with a cone shape

2.2.6

8 Lee is using these materials to conduct an investigation.

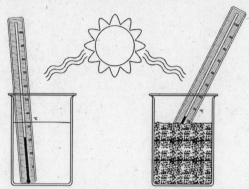

Which question can he MOST LIKELY answer from this investigation?

○ Does the sun warm soil more than it warms water?

○ Does the sun warm water more than it warms air?

○ How does the sun cause water to evaporate?

2.2.5

9 You and your classmates set a cup of soil and a cup of water in the sun. You measure and record the temperature of the soil and the water. What should you do NEXT?

○ ask a question

○ compare results

○ explain what happened

2.2.5

10 What do we call moving air that surrounds us?

○ clouds

○ rain

○ wind

2.2.2

11 You want to make a rain gauge. Which object would work the BEST?

○ a glass bowl

○ a paper bag

○ a plastic bottle

2.2.1

12 Which type of clouds would you MOST LIKELY see on a bright and sunny day?

○ cumulonimbus

○ cumulus

○ stratus

2.2.3

13 You observe the weather for a week. What is the BEST way for you to record your observations?

○ talk to a friend about what you observe

○ think about what you observe

○ write or draw what you observe

2.2.3

14 Why do meteorologists try to predict severe weather?

○ to name storms

○ to stop severe weather

○ to warn people about severe weather

2.2.6

15 You observe the weather for five days and make this chart.

Monday	Tuesday	Wednesday	Thursday	Friday
cloudy	rain	sunny	cloudy	rain

Which can you conclude?

○ On days when it rained, the day before was cloudy.

○ It was sunny on more days than it was cloudy.

○ The weather on Saturday will also be rainy.

2.2.3, 2.2.4

16 Tom sets a cup of soil and a cup of water in the sun. After an hour, the soil has a higher temperature than the water. What can Tom infer, or figure out, from this activity?

○ The soil feels warmer than the water.

○ Land takes in more energy from the sun than water does.

○ Water takes in more energy from the sun than land does.

2.2.5

17 This chart shows one town's average temperatures for four months of the year.

February	May	September	December
35 °F	65 °F	70 °F	37 °F

Which is TRUE?

○ December has the coldest average temperature.

○ May has the warmest average temperature.

○ September has the warmest average temperature.

2.2.4

18 What happens to the girl's shadow as the day goes from early afternoon to late afternoon?

○ The position of her shadow changes.

○ The size of her shadow changes.

○ Both the position and the size of her shadow changes.

2.2.7

19 Which is TRUE about the moon?

○ The moon can only be seen at night.

○ The moon reflects light from the sun.

○ The moon shines with its own light.

2.2.8

20 About how much time passes from one new moon to the next new moon?

○ a month

○ a week

○ a year

2.2.9

Weather Watcher

Materials

construction paper   crayons or markers   pencil

Procedure

You will make a book to record what the wind is like for one week. Follow these steps.

❶ Fold three sheets of paper in half. Write "Weather Watcher" on the cover. Write the days on the five pages.

❷ Go outside each day. Write whether the wind is blowing, and tell how you know.

❸ Write about what the wind is like.

❹ Share your book with the class. Compare your book with classmates' books. Talk about how the books are alike and different.

Weather Watcher

Materials Performance Task sheets, construction paper, crayons or markers, pencils

Time 25 minutes the first and last days; 10–15 minutes the other days

Suggested Grouping individuals or pairs

Inquiry Skills observe, communicate, compare

Preparation Hints Show children how to fold three sheets of construction paper in half to make a 6-page book. Staple the pages on the fold. Have children write *Weather Watcher* on the cover and label each page with the name of the school day.

Introduce the Task Review with the children different ways you can tell whether the wind is blowing. Invite volunteers to suggest words that children could use to describe the wind, for example, *calm, blowing a little, blowing hard, strong*. Distribute the Performance Task sheets, and ask children to read the directions aloud with you. Answer any questions that children raise.

Promote Discussion Ask children to name ways the wind affects them in their everyday lives, for example, by enabling them to fly kites.

Scoring Rubric

Performance Indicators
_____ Records whether the wind is blowing each day.
_____ Records how he or she knows whether the wind is blowing.
_____ Describes the wind each day with appropriate words.
_____ Compares and discusses findings with others.
Observations and Rubric Score
3   **2**   **1**   **0**

What Are Some Animal Life Cycles?

❶ Which picture shows a tadpole?

Ⓐ

Ⓑ

Ⓒ

❷ Which of these animals is born live?

Ⓐ an eagle

Ⓑ a frog

Ⓒ a tiger

❸ Which stage of a butterfly's life cycle does the picture show?

Ⓐ an egg

Ⓑ a larva

Ⓒ a pupa

❹ How is a butterfly's life cycle different from a bird's life cycle?

Ⓐ A butterfly goes through metamorphosis.

Ⓑ A butterfly hatches from an egg.

Ⓒ A butterfly looks like its parents when it is born.

How Does a Bean Plant Grow?

1 What can you infer about a bean plant that gets light, water, and air?

Ⓐ It will die.

Ⓑ It will grow well.

Ⓒ It will not grow well.

2 Jana did an experiment with two plants. She gave fresh water to one plant and salt water to the other plant. The plant that was given salt water did not grow well.

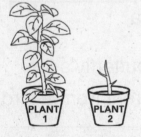

PLANT 1   PLANT 2

Which can you conclude?

Ⓐ Plant 1 was given fresh water.

Ⓑ Plant 1 was given salt water.

Ⓒ Plant 2 was given fresh water.

3 What can you observe about a bean seed by using a hand lens?

Ⓐ the details of the bean seed

Ⓑ the way the bean seed feels

Ⓒ the way the bean seed smells

4 Which is something you can observe with your senses alone?

Ⓐ Bean plants need water to grow.

Ⓑ Bean plants need sunlight to grow.

Ⓒ Bean plants have green leaves.

What Are Some Plant Life Cycles?

❶ Which part of a plant holds seeds?

- Ⓐ a fruit
- Ⓑ a leaf
- Ⓒ a stem

❷ Which is the **first** thing that grows from a seed?

- Ⓐ flowers
- Ⓑ leaves
- Ⓒ roots

❸ Which picture shows an adult plant?

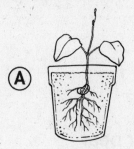

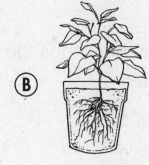

❹ How does a cone help a pine tree during its life cycle?

- Ⓐ A cone grows flowers.
- Ⓑ A cone makes fruit.
- Ⓒ A cone holds and protects seeds.

Life Cycles

1 The snake is hatching from an egg. Which animal's life cycle is MOST similar to the snake's life cycle?

- ○ a bird
- ○ a cat
- ○ a polar bear

2.3.1, 2.3.2

2 Which term describes the changes an animal goes through as it grows?

- ○ animal cycle
- ○ life cycle
- ○ water cycle

2.3.1

3 Which animal goes through metamorphosis during its life cycle?

- ○ a dolphin
- ○ a frog
- ○ a monkey

2.3.2

4 Which stage comes FIRST in a polar bear's life cycle?

- ○ adult
- ○ cub
- ○ newborn

2.3.1

5 What do seeds need in order to germinate?

○ water

○ shade

○ food

2.3.1

6 In which stage of a plant's life cycle do leaves FIRST appear?

○ adult

○ seed

○ seedling

2.3.1

7 Which part of a plant's life cycle is shown?

○ adult

○ seed

○ seedling

2.3.1

8 What kind of life cycle is shown here?

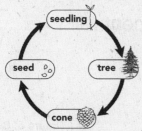

○ the life cycle of a bean plant

○ the life cycle of a pine tree

○ the life cycle of an apple tree

2.3.1, 2.3.2

9 Jamal observes these two plants. He knows the plants are the same kind of plant. He knows the seeds they grew from were planted on the same day. He infers that Plant 2 received more warmth, air, and water than Plant 1. Why does he infer this?

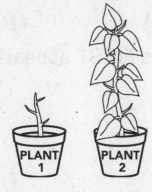

○ Plant 2 grew in the same way as Plant 1.

○ Plant 2 is shorter and has fewer leaves than Plant 1.

○ Plant 2 is taller and has more leaves than Plant 1.

Nature of Science

10 Ana planted two bean seeds. She kept one in a warm, light environment. She kept the other in a cold, dark environment. Which bean seed will MOST LIKELY grow better?

○ The bean seed in the warm, light environment will grow better.

○ The bean seed in the cold, dark environment will grow better.

○ Both bean seeds will grow the same way.

Nature of Science

11 Three bean seeds were planted at the same time.

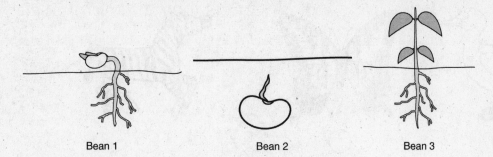

Bean 1   Bean 2   Bean 3

Which one grew MOST SLOWLY?

○ Bean 1

○ Bean 2

○ Bean 3

2.3.2

12 How is a peach different from a pinecone?

○ A peach holds seeds.

○ A peach is a cone.

○ A peach is a fruit.

2.3.2

13 How can you tell that the seeds in the cup have germinated?

○ They have grown flowers.

○ They have grown out of the cup.

○ They have roots and small leaves.

Nature of Science

14 Which animal looks different from its parent when it is born?

○   ○   ○

2.3.1, 2.3.2

15 Which animal hatches from an egg?

○ a lion

○ a rabbit

○ a turtle

2.3.2

16 Which is the correct order of the butterfly life cycle?

○ adult, pupa, egg, larva

○ egg, larva, pupa, adult

○ egg, pupa, larva, adult

2.3.1

17 Which is TRUE?

○ An adult frog can live on land only.

○ An adult frog uses gills to take in oxygen.

○ A tadpole loses its tail before becoming an adult frog.

2.3.1

18 How are plants and animals alike?

○ They begin their life cycles as seeds.

○ They go through metamorphosis.

○ They grow and change during their life cycles.

2.3.2

19 Which is a cone?

○   ○   ○

2.3.2

20 Which is TRUE about this kind of animal?

○ Its young are born live.

○ Its young hatch from eggs.

○ This kind of animal does not reproduce.

2.3.1

How Plants Grow

Materials

construction paper   markers or crayons   writing paper   pencil

Procedure

Teach your class about plants. Choose one of these lessons.

Lesson 1   Tell how a seed becomes a plant.

Lesson 2   Tell how the different parts of a plant help it grow.

❶ Make a list of words that will help you tell about plants. Use these words to write what you will say.

❷ Draw a picture that will help you teach your lesson.

> ### Lesson Words
> 1. stems
> 2. leaves
> 3. roots
> 4. seeds
> 5. sunlight

❸ If you choose Lesson 1, add labels that explain the order in which things happen.

❹ If you choose Lesson 2, add labels that name the parts of a plant.

❺ Use your picture as you teach your lesson to the class.

How Plants Grow

Materials Performance Task sheets, construction paper, markers or crayons, writing paper, pencils

Time 25 minutes for children to prepare their lessons

Suggested Grouping individuals

Inquiry Skills classify, communicate, sequence

Preparation Hints none

Introduce the Task Review the two topics with children, and make sure they understand that they should choose just one. Have a volunteer read the partial list of terms, and invite children to add to that list. Distribute the Performance Task sheets and materials, and ask children to read the directions aloud with you. Clarify that Steps 3 and 4 give two sets of directions, one for each topic, and that they will follow only the set for the topic they choose. Answer any questions that children raise.

Promote Discussion Ask children to use their drawings and labels to explain their topic. Invite volunteers to use their drawings to explain other topics about plants, such as how to grow new plants.

Scoring Rubric

Performance Indicators
_____ Makes accurate drawings of plant parts or a plant life cycle.
_____ Labels drawings correctly.
_____ Uses proper sequence to explain a plant's life cycle or accurate terms to identify plant parts and tell what they do.
_____ Communicates information about the chosen topic to the whole class.

Observations and Rubric Score
3   **2**   **1**   **0**

How Are Body Parts Like Tools?

❶ How are your teeth and an ax alike?

Ⓐ Both are soft.

Ⓑ Both cut and chop.

Ⓒ Both twist and bend.

❷ How is this person using his hands as tools?

Ⓐ to cut

Ⓑ to fold

Ⓒ to pull

❸ Why do engineers make artificial body parts?

Ⓐ to build models of real people

Ⓑ to see how real body parts work

Ⓒ to help people who are missing a body part

❹ Janie has an artificial hand. What can this help her do?

Ⓐ grab and hold things

Ⓑ run

Ⓒ swim faster

What Is the Design Process?

❶ Which process uses math and science to help you solve a problem?

(A) the design process

(B) the engineer process

(C) the problem method

❷ What do engineers do after they plan a solution and choose materials?

(A) brainstorm ideas

(B) build the solution

(C) test the solution

❸ Why do engineers follow the design process?

(A) to make problems

(B) to solve problems

(C) to talk about problems

❹ Leo made a robot to pick up his dirty laundry. Which step in the design process would tell him his plan worked?

(A) Plan a solution.

(B) Build the solution.

(C) Test the solution.

How Can We Use the Design Process?

1 The picture shows Mandy's plan to keep birds out of her dad's garden.

What materials will she choose?

Ⓐ old clothes and string

Ⓑ paper and tape

Ⓒ steel and concrete

2 Why is it **best** to test your solution more than once?

Ⓐ to make sure it works

Ⓑ to use more materials

Ⓒ to think of new problems

3 Marc's little sister cannot reach the sink to brush her teeth. What does Marc plan to build to solve her problem?

Ⓐ a booster seat

Ⓑ a taller sink

Ⓒ a step stool

4 Alicia is thinking about ways to move a heavy box of books. What should she do next?

Ⓐ build a solution

Ⓑ communicate her results

Ⓒ plan a solution

Designs to Meet Needs

1 Which body part works like an oar when you swim?

- ○ an arm
- ○ a head
- ○ a leg

2.4.1

2 What body parts do you use to cut food?

- ○ arms
- ○ feet
- ○ teeth

2.4.1

3 How is the boy using his hand and arm as a tool?

- ○ to cut something
- ○ to hold something
- ○ to turn something

2.4.1

4 Which kind of tool works MOST LIKE teeth?

○ a hammer

○ a knife

○ pliers

2.4.1

5 Some engineers make artificial legs. Who will an artificial leg help?

○ a person who is missing a leg

○ a person who likes to be active

○ a person who uses body parts as tools

2.4.2

6 Which tool is MOST LIKE an artificial hand?

○ an ax

○ an oar

○ pliers

2.4.1

7 An arm lifts things. Which tool is MOST LIKE an arm?

 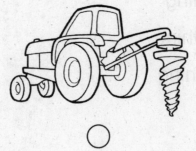 

○ ○ ○

2.4.1

8 How do engineers use math and science in their work?

○ to read books

○ to solve problems

○ to write letters

Design Process

Use this information to answer questions 9–13.

Abby had a problem. She followed steps to solve her problem. She made this fan.

9 What was Abby's problem?

○ Abby was cold.

○ Abby was hot.

○ Abby was wet.

Design Process, 2.4.3

10 What material did Abby MOST LIKELY use to make her fan?

○ cloth

○ paper

○ wood

Design Process, 2.4.3

11 To solve her problem, Abby used the same process engineers use to solve problems. What process did she follow?

- ○ the design process
- ○ the fan process
- ○ the work process

J Design Process, 2.4.3

12 What should Abby do to find out if her fan solves the problem?

- ○ ask a friend
- ○ keep good records
- ○ test her solution

J Design Process, 2.4.3

13 What can Abby's friend do to make the same fan?

- ○ draw a different plan
- ○ follow Abby's plan
- ○ look for a new problem

J Design Process, 2.4.3

Use this information to answer questions 14–17.

Hugo's books make his backpack too heavy to carry. He uses the design process to find a solution to get his books to school.

14 Hugo brainstorms ideas. What should he do next?

- ○ build a solution
- ○ keep good records
- ○ test the solution

J Design Process, 2.4.3

15 This is Hugo's backpack. His ideas are to use hooks, rope, or wheels to move the backpack. Which idea will MOST LIKELY solve his problem?

○ hooks

○ rope

○ wheels

Design Process, 2.4.3

16 Who should test Hugo's solution?

○ an engineer

○ Hugo

○ Hugo's teacher

Design Process, 2.4.3

17 What should Hugo do if his solution does not work?

○ buy a bigger backpack

○ make a new plan and try again

○ stop taking his books to school

Design Process, 2.4.3

Use this picture to answer questions 18–20.

18 Which step of the design process does the picture show?

○ Find a problem.

○ Plan a solution and choose materials.

○ Build the solution.

Design Process, 2.4.2

19 What problem are the engineers solving in the picture?

○ Our town needs a new bridge.

○ Our town needs a new park.

○ Our town needs a new school.

Design Process, 2.4.2

20 Which of these steps happened BEFORE the other two steps?

○ The materials were chosen.

○ The results were communicated.

○ The solution was built.

Design Process, 2.4.2

Organize Your Classroom Library

Materials

cardboard box

construction paper

scissors

markers

Procedure

1 Brainstorm ways to organize the books in your classroom library.

2 Keep good records.

3 Draw a design for a model of your solution. Choose your materials.

4 Build your model.

5 Test it.

6 Communicate your findings with the class.

Organize Your Classroom Library

Materials Performance Task sheets, cardboard,
building materials, construction paper, scissors, markers

Time 45 minutes

Suggested Grouping small groups

Inquiry Skills make a model, communicate

Preparation Hints Have all of the materials measured and pre-cut so that children can spend more time assembling their models.

Introduce the Task Prompt children to think about their classroom library. Guide children in understanding how their library is organized. Review the steps of the design process with children. Distribute the Performance Task sheets, and ask children to read the steps of the procedure aloud with you. Answer any questions that children raise.

Promote Discussion Lead children in a discussion about why it is important to organize their classroom library. Elicit from them ways they could organize it better. Brainstorm ideas, and then have the class decide on one design.

Scoring Rubric

Performance Indicators
_____ Plans and builds a solution.
_____ Tests the solution.
_____ Keeps good records and communicates results with classmates.
Observations and Rubric Score
3   2   1   0

1 What happens when an ice cube melts?

○ It changes from a liquid to a gas.

○ It changes from a liquid to a solid.

○ It changes from a solid to a liquid.

2.1.1

2 Which is an example of a mixture?

○ a carrot

○ salt

○ vegetable soup

2.1.2

3 You put equal amounts of sand and water in this beaker. Then you place the beaker in a warm location.

What will you MOST LIKELY observe after two days?

○ The amounts of sand and water are still the same.

○ There is less sand than water.

○ There is less water than sand.

Nature of Science, 2.1.3

4 Mr. Lee wants to travel from one town to another town across the country. Which would be the FASTEST way for him to travel?

○ flying by plane

○ riding a bike

○ walking

2.1.4

5 Where is the boy holding the ball?

○ above his head

○ behind his back

○ in front of his chest

2.1.5

6 How can you make an object move TOWARD you?

○ pull it

○ push it

○ throw it

2.1.6

7 Look at this picture.

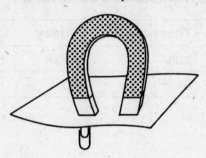

What is happening?

○ The magnet is attracting the paper clip.

○ The magnet is attracting the sheet of paper.

○ The sheet of paper is attracting the paper clip.

2.1.7

8 What can you measure with this tool?

○ rainfall

○ temperature

○ wind direction

2.2.1

9 Which is TRUE?

○ Wind is a type of precipitation.

○ Wind is air that stays still.

○ Wind is air that is moving.

2.2.2

10 You observe the weather for five days and make this chart.

Monday	Tuesday	Wednesday	Thursday	Friday
rain	sunny	mostly cloudy	rain	snow
36 °F	40 °F	38 °F	34 °F	30 °F

Which observation is CORRECT?

○ It was coldest during sunny weather.

○ On Friday, the temperature was lower than on the days that it rained.

○ The temperature was the same on the two rainy days.

2.2.3, 2.2.4

11 Ben has two beakers. One beaker is empty and one beaker has water in it. He puts a thermometer in each beaker and puts the beakers out in the sun. What is he MOST LIKELY investigating?

○ how the sun heats air and water

○ how the sun heats water and soil

○ how the sun heats water only

2.2.5

12 Which scientists warn people about severe weather?

○ botanists

○ meteorologists

○ zoologists

2.2.6

13 What time of day does this picture show?

○ afternoon

○ early morning

○ night

2.2.7

14 Which is TRUE about the moon?

○ It heats Earth.

○ It is a star.

○ It seems to rise at night.

2.2.8

15 Which is the correct order of the phases of the moon?

○ first quarter moon, third quarter moon, full moon, new moon

○ full moon, first quarter moon, new moon, third quarter moon

○ new moon, first quarter moon, full moon, third quarter moon

2.2.9

16 Which animal looks like its parents when it is born?

○ a butterfly

○ a frog

○ a giraffe

2.3.1, 2.3.2

17 How is an apple tree DIFFERENT from a pine tree?

○ An apple tree grows fruits that hold seeds.

○ An apple tree has cones that hold seeds.

○ An apple tree makes seeds.

2.3.1, 2.3.2

18 Which picture shows how you can use your hand like a tool?

○   ○   ○

2.4.1

19 How is an artificial arm DIFFERENT from a real arm?

○ An artificial arm can help a person do things.

○ An artificial arm is covered with skin.

○ An artificial arm is made from human-made materials.

2.4.2

20 Tyra built a basket to put on her bike. Which step of the design process should she do AFTER she tests the basket?

○ communicate the results of the test

○ record her brainstorming ideas

○ think about the results of the test

Design Process, 2.4.3

Name _____ Date _____

ISTEP+ Practice Test A

Mark one answer for each question.

1 ◯ ◯ ◯   **11** ◯ ◯ ◯

2 ◯ ◯ ◯   **12** ◯ ◯ ◯

3 ◯ ◯ ◯   **13** ◯ ◯ ◯

4 ◯ ◯ ◯   **14** ◯ ◯ ◯

5 ◯ ◯ ◯   **15** ◯ ◯ ◯

6 ◯ ◯ ◯   **16** ◯ ◯ ◯

7 ◯ ◯ ◯   **17** ◯ ◯ ◯

8 ◯ ◯ ◯   **18** ◯ ◯ ◯

9 ◯ ◯ ◯   **19** ◯ ◯ ◯

10 ◯ ◯ ◯   **20** ◯ ◯ ◯

❶ When does water become solid?

○ when it evaporates

○ when it freezes

○ when it melts

⬤ 2.1.1

❷ Bree is conducting an investigation using salt, a beaker of water, and a clock.

Which question is she MOST LIKELY trying to answer?

○ How long does it take for salt to dissolve in water?

○ Why does salt dissolve in water?

○ Will salt dissolve in oil?

⬤ **Nature of Science, 2.1.2**

❸ Mrs. Adler boils vegetables in a pot of water. Why does steam come out of the pot?

○ Some of the water is evaporating.

○ Some of the vegetables are dissolving.

○ Some of the vegetables are evaporating.

⬤ 2.1.3

4 How is the skier moving?

- ◯ back and forth
- ◯ in a circle
- ◯ in a straight line

2.1.4

5 What is an object's position?

- ◯ how fast the object is moving
- ◯ where the object is located
- ◯ which way the object is moving

2.1.5

6 The girl pulls the wagon. What happens?

- ◯ The wagon moves away from her.
- ◯ The wagon moves toward her.
- ◯ The wagon stops moving.

2.1.6

7 Two magnets are moving AWAY from each other. What is happening?

○ Opposite magnetic poles are attracting each other.

○ Opposite magnetic poles are repelling each other.

○ The same magnetic poles are repelling each other.

2.1.7

8 Which is TRUE?

○ A rain gauge measures precipitation.

○ A thermometer measures wind direction.

○ A weather vane measures precipitation.

2.2.1

9 How are these objects ALIKE?

○ They measure precipitation.

○ The wind makes them move.

○ They are weather vanes.

2.2.2

10 Pedro observed the weather for five days and made this chart.

Monday	Tuesday	Wednesday	Thursday	Friday
cumulus clouds	cumulus clouds	stratus clouds	cirrus clouds	stratus clouds

Which can you INFER from this information?

○ It rained every day that Pedro observed the weather.

○ Pedro observed sunny weather on some of the days.

○ The temperature was highest on Thursday.

2.2.3, 2.2.4

11 You and your classmates are investigating how the sun heats soil and water. You set a cup of soil and a cup of water in the sun. What will you MOST LIKELY observe after one hour?

○ The temperature of the soil is higher than the temperature of the water.

○ The temperature of the water is higher than the temperature of the soil.

○ The temperatures of the soil and of the water are still the same.

2.2.5

12 Which is a way you can prepare for a severe storm?

○ go outside to watch the storm

○ stock up on food and water

○ take pictures of the storm

2.2.6

13 You measure your shadow in the morning. By noon, you observe that your shadow is shorter and the position has changed. Why did your shadow change?

○ Earth moved.

○ The moon moved.

○ The sun moved.

2.2.7

14 How is the moon DIFFERENT from the sun?

○ The moon can be seen at night.

○ The moon is always in the same place in the sky.

○ The moon seems to rise in the morning.

2.2.8

15 Which phase of the moon does number 5 show?

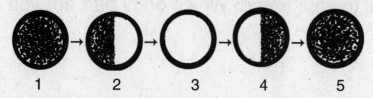

1   2   3   4   5

○ first quarter moon

○ full moon

○ new moon

2.2.9

16 How are a tadpole and a caterpillar ALIKE?

- ◯ Both live in water.
- ◯ Both look different from their parents.
- ◯ Both will grow wings before becoming an adult.

2.3.1, 2.3.2

17 Which picture shows a fruit?

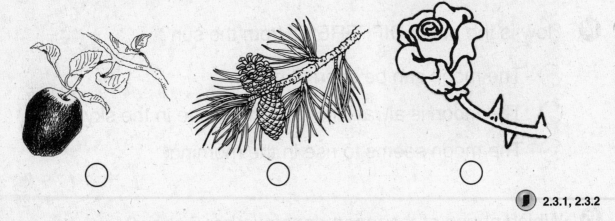

◯   ◯   ◯

2.3.1, 2.3.2

18 You throw a baseball to your friend. Which body part are you using like a tool?

- ◯ your arm
- ◯ your foot
- ◯ your teeth

2.4.1

19 Which is TRUE about artificial body parts?

○ All artificial body parts look like real body parts.

○ All artificial body parts are covered with skin.

○ Artificial body parts take the place of some real body parts.

2.4.2

20 Ken designed and built a running wheel for his pet hamster. Which step of the design process should he do NEXT?

○ Brainstorm ideas.

○ Plan a solution.

○ Test the solution.

Design Process, 2.4.3

Name _____ Date _____

ISTEP+ Practice Test B

Mark one answer for each question.

1 ○ ○ ○　　**11** ○ ○ ○

2 ○ ○ ○　　**12** ○ ○ ○

3 ○ ○ ○　　**13** ○ ○ ○

4 ○ ○ ○　　**14** ○ ○ ○

5 ○ ○ ○　　**15** ○ ○ ○

6 ○ ○ ○　　**16** ○ ○ ○

7 ○ ○ ○　　**17** ○ ○ ○

8 ○ ○ ○　　**18** ○ ○ ○

9 ○ ○ ○　　**19** ○ ○ ○

10 ○ ○ ○　　**20** ○ ○ ○

❶ What is condensation?

○ the change of water from a gas to a liquid

○ the change of water from a liquid to a gas

○ the change of water from a liquid to a solid

2.1.1

❷ You put sand in a cup of water. What will happen to the sand?

○ It will dissolve in the water.

○ It will evaporate from the cup.

○ It will sink to the bottom of the cup.

2.1.2

❸ Which mixture would you MOST LIKELY use a sieve to separate?

○ rice and water

○ water and salt

○ white rice and brown rice

2.1.3

❹ Which object rolls?

○ a ball

○ a book

○ a box

2.1.4

5 Which words can be used to describe an object's position?

○ above, below

○ fast, slow

○ pull, push

2.1.5

6 What are the boy and the man BOTH doing?

○ pulling an object

○ pushing an object

○ putting force on an object

2.1.6

7 Look at the picture. The girl is holding a rope and jumping over it.

What happens NEXT?

○ Gravity holds her up in the air.

○ Gravity pulls her down to the ground.

○ Gravity pulls the rope down to the ground.

2.1.7

❽ Which tool can you make to measure precipitation?

○ a rain gauge

○ a thermometer

○ a weather vane

2.2.1

❾ Which picture shows how wind can move a tree?

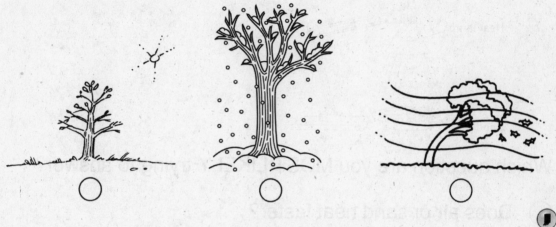

○　　　　　　○　　　　　　○

2.2.2

❿ Bella observed the weather for five days and made this chart.

Monday	Tuesday	Wednesday	Thursday	Friday
snow—4 inches	mostly cloudy	sunny	rain—1 inch	rain—1 inch

Which can Bella CONCLUDE about these five days?

○ The amount of rainfall was greater than the amount of snowfall.

○ The amount of snowfall was greater than the amount of rainfall.

○ The amount of rainfall and the amount of snowfall were the same.

2.2.3, 2.2.4

11 You and your classmates are doing an investigation with the materials shown here.

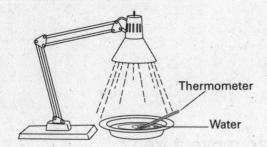

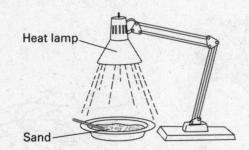

Which question are you MOST LIKELY trying to answer?

○ Does air or sand heat faster?

○ Does sand or water heat faster?

○ How does wind move sand and water?

Nature of Science, 2.2.5

12 Where is the safest place to be during a severe storm?

○ inside, away from any windows

○ inside, by a window

○ outside, under a tree

2.2.6

13 Sam has a tree in his backyard. He observes and draws the tree's shadow every three hours for one day. What will his observations show?

○ The shadow is always in front of the tree.

○ The shadow is to the left of the tree all day.

○ The shadow's position changes throughout the day.

2.2.7

14 What time of day does this picture show?

○ afternoon

○ morning

○ night

2.2.8

15 Which is TRUE?

○ A full moon can be seen only once a year.

○ The pattern of the moon's phases lasts about a month.

○ The third quarter moon phase lasts about a month.

2.2.9

16 How is a frog's life cycle DIFFERENT from a turtle's life cycle?

○ A frog goes through metamorphosis during its life cycle.

○ A frog hatches from an egg.

○ A frog looks like its parents when it is born.

2.3.1, 2.3.2

17 Which picture shows an adult living thing?

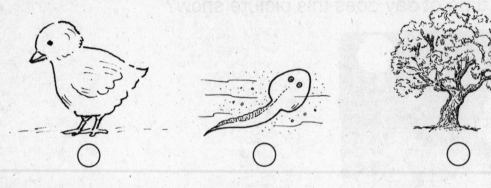

○   ○   ○

2.3.1, 2.3.2

18 How are teeth and a knife ALIKE?

○ They are body parts.

○ They can cut food.

○ They can grab things.

2.4.1

19 What does **artificial** mean?

○ found in nature

○ made by humans

○ made from metal

2.4.2

20 Debra cannot reach things on the top shelf of her closet. She wants to solve this problem using the design process. What should she do FIRST?

○ brainstorm ideas

○ build the solution

○ choose materials

Design Process, 2.4.3

Name _____ Date _____

ISTEP+ Practice Test C

Mark one answer for each question.

1 ○ ○ ○   **11** ○ ○ ○

2 ○ ○ ○   **12** ○ ○ ○

3 ○ ○ ○   **13** ○ ○ ○

4 ○ ○ ○   **14** ○ ○ ○

5 ○ ○ ○   **15** ○ ○ ○

6 ○ ○ ○   **16** ○ ○ ○

7 ○ ○ ○   **17** ○ ○ ○

8 ○ ○ ○   **18** ○ ○ ○

9 ○ ○ ○   **19** ○ ○ ○

10 ○ ○ ○   **20** ○ ○ ○

Unit 1 The Practice of Science

Lesson 1 Quiz, p. AG 1
1. B
2. A
3. B
4. A

Lesson 2 Quiz, p. AG 2
1. C
2. A
3. B
4. A

Lesson 3 Quiz, p. AG 3
1. A
2. A
3. B
4. B

Lesson 4 Quiz, p. AG 4
1. A
2. B
3. C
4. C

Lesson 5 Quiz, p. AG 5
1. A
2. C
3. A
4. A

Unit 1 Test and ISTEP+ Practice, pp. AG 6–11
1. comparing
2. a measuring cup
3. the hand lens
4. You do the same thing to each part being tested.
5. predicting
6. make a statement that you can test
7. a measuring cup
8. to classify the rocks
9. a thermometer
10. a tape measure
11. Their data will be the same.
12. repeat the test
13. It is based on the data.
14. The ball moved fast.
15. a plan for making something
16. a basketball
17. A model can show how parts fit together.
18. They show what happens first, next, and last.
19. Are the birds looking for worms to eat?
20. You form a conclusion about what you learned from a test.

Unit 2 Matter

Lesson 1 Quiz, p. AG 14
1. C
2. B
3. C
4. A

Lesson 2 Quiz, p. AG 15
1. B
2. C
3. A
4. A

Lesson 3 Quiz, p. AG 16
1. B
2. C
3. B
4. B

Lesson 4 Quiz, p. AG 17
1. C
2. C
3. A
4. B

Lesson 5 Quiz, p. AG 18
1. A
2. C
3. C
4. C

Unit 2 Test and ISTEP+ Practice, pp. AG 19–24
1. The air takes the shape of the balloon.
2. mass
3. picture of the raindrops
4. water vapor
5. ice cubes
6. It is melting.
7. It changes shape.
8. The puddles evaporated.
9. The temperature got lower.
10. The water expanded and changed the shape of the bottle.
11. heat it on the stove
12. breaking a pencil
13. the sugar
14. The salt dissolves.
15. write about your results
16. to separate the noodles from the water
17. use evaporation to separate the drink powder from the water
18. beads and water
19. evaporate the water
20. evaporate the water

Unit 3 Motion and Forces

Lesson 1 Quiz, p. AG 27
1. B
2. C
3. A
4. C

Lesson 2 Quiz, p. AG 28
1. C
2. A
3. B
4. B

Lesson 3 Quiz, p. AG 29
1. B
2. A
3. B
4. C

Lesson 4 Quiz, p. AG 30
1. A
2. B
3. C
4. C

Lesson 5 Quiz, p. AG 31
1. B
2. C
3. C
4. A

Lesson 6 Quiz, p. AG 32
1. C
2. B
3. A
4. B

Unit 4 Weather and the Sky

Lesson 1 Quiz, p. AG 41
1. B
2. C
3. C
4. A

Lesson 2 Quiz, p. AG 42
1. C
2. B
3. B
4. A

Lesson 3 Quiz, p. AG 43
1. C
2. B
3. C
4. B

Lesson 4 Quiz, p. AG 44
1. B
2. A
3. C
4. C

Lesson 5 Quiz, p. AG 45
1. A
2. C
3. A
4. B

Lesson 6 Quiz, p. AG 46
1. C
2. A
3. C
4. B

Unit 3 Test and ISTEP+ Practice, pp. AG 33–38
1. fast
2. a train
3. speed
4. a force
5. sight and hearing
6. a slide
7. talk about what you see
8. round and round
9. push it
10. draw or write about it
11. back and forth
12. He is moving it out of the truck.
13. a pull
14. You can investigate.
15. How can I make a ball move?
16. your foot
17. Gravity pulls the ball to the ground.
18. The desk holds it up.
19. steel nails
20. Different magnetic poles are attracting each other.

Unit 4 Test and ISTEP+ Practice, pp. AG 47–52

1. the picture of a sailboat
2. snowy and cold
3. a thermometer
4. the picture of the weather vane
5. summer
6. stay indoors
7. heavy rain and strong winds
8. Does the sun warm soil more than it warms water?
9. compare results
10. wind
11. a plastic bottle
12. cumulus
13. write or draw what you observe
14. to warn people about severe weather
15. On days when it rained, the day before was cloudy.
16. Land takes in more energy from the sun than water does.
17. September has the warmest average temperature.
18. Both the position and the size of her shadow changes.
19. The moon reflects light from the sun.
20. a month

Unit 5 Life Cycles

Lesson 1 Quiz, p. AG 55
1. B
2. C
3. C
4. A

Lesson 2 Quiz, p. AG 56
1. B
2. A
3. A
4. C

Lesson 3 Quiz, p. AG 57
1. A
2. C
3. B
4. C

Unit 5 Test and ISTEP+ Practice, pp. AG 58–63

1. a bird
2. life cycle
3. a frog
4. newborn
5. water
6. seedling
7. seedling
8. the life cycle of a pine tree
9. Plant 2 is taller and has more leaves than Plant 1.
10. The bean seed in the warm, light environment will grow better.
11. Bean 2
12. A peach is a fruit.
13. They have roots and small leaves.
14. the picture of the butterfly
15. a turtle
16. egg, larva, pupa, adult
17. A tadpole loses its tail before becoming an adult frog.
18. They grow and change during their life cycles.
19. the picture of the pinecone
20. Its young are born live.

Unit 6 Designs to Meet Needs

Lesson 1 Quiz, p. AG 66
1. B
2. B
3. C
4. A

Lesson 2 Quiz, p. AG 67
1. A
2. B
3. B
4. C

Lesson 3 Quiz, p. AG 68
1. A
2. A
3. C
4. C

Unit 6 Test and ISTEP+ Practice, pp. AG 69–74

1. an arm
2. teeth
3. to hold something
4. a knife
5. a person who is missing a leg
6. pliers
7. picture of the tow truck
8. to solve problems
9. Abby was hot.
10. paper
11. the design process
12. test her solution
13. follow Abby's plan
14. keep good records
15. wheels
16. Hugo
17. make a new plan and try again
18. Build the solution.
19. Our town needs a new school.
20. The materials were chosen.

ISTEP+ Practice Test A pp. AG 77–83

1. It changes from a solid to a liquid.
2. vegetable soup
3. There is less water than sand.
4. flying by plane
5. behind his back
6. pull it
7. The magnet is attracting the paper clip.
8. temperature
9. Wind is air that is moving.
10. On Friday, the temperature was lower than on the days that it rained.
11. how the sun heats air and water
12. meteorologists
13. early morning
14. It seems to rise at night.
15. new moon, first quarter moon, full moon, third quarter moon
16. a giraffe
17. An apple tree grows fruits that hold seeds.
18. Picture 2
19. An artificial arm is made from human-made materials.
20. communicate the results of the test

ISTEP+ Practice Test B pp. AG 85–91

1. when it freezes
2. How long does it take for salt to dissolve in water?
3. Some of the water is evaporating.
4. in a straight line
5. where the object is located
6. The wagon moves toward her.
7. The same magnetic poles are repelling each other.
8. A rain gauge measures precipitation.
9. The wind makes them move.
10. Pedro observed sunny weather on some of the days.
11. The temperature of the soil is higher than the temperature of the water.
12. stock up on food and water
13. Earth moved.
14. The moon can be seen at night.
15. a new moon
16. Both look different from their parents.
17. Picture 1
18. your arm
19. Artificial body parts take the place of some real body parts.
20. Test the solution.

ISTEP+ Practice Test C pp. AG 93–99

1. the change of water from a gas to a liquid
2. It will sink to the bottom of the cup.
3. rice and water
4. a ball
5. above; below
6. putting force on an object
7. Gravity pulls her down to the ground.
8. a rain gauge
9. Picture 3
10. The amount of snowfall was greater than the amount of rainfall.
11. Does sand or water heat faster?
12. inside, away from any windows
13. The shadow's position changes throughout the day.
14. night
15. The pattern of the moon's phases lasts about a month.
16. A frog goes through metamorphosis during its life cycle.
17. Picture 3 (adult tree)
18. They can cut food.
19. made by humans
20. brainstorm ideas